I0410881

U.S. Department of the Interior
Office of Inspector General

Collection of Outstanding Taxes and Fees
Government of the Virgin Islands

Report No. V-IN-VIS-0011-2006   **January 2008**

United States Department of the Interior

OFFICE OF INSPECTOR GENERAL
Western Region Office
2800 Cottage Way, Suite E-2712
Sacramento, California 95825

January 10, 2008

Honorable John P. de Jongh, Jr.
Governor of the Virgin Islands
No. 21 Kongens Gade
St. Thomas, VI 00802

Re: Final Audit Report *Collection of Outstanding Taxes and Fees, Government of the Virgin Islands* (Report No. V-IN-VIS-0011-2006)

Dear Governor de Jongh:

The enclosed final report presents the results of our audit of the collection of outstanding taxes and fees of the Government of the Virgin Islands (GVI). Our objective was to evaluate the current level of taxes and fees owed to GVI and determine whether GVI was making reasonable efforts to collect these outstanding amounts. Our audit scope and methodology are detailed in Appendix 1.

We found that the process of collecting delinquent taxes in the Virgin Islands is inefficient and ineffectual and does not fully comply with the law. The Bureau of Internal Revenue (BIR) and the Department of Finance (DOF) did not act in the best interest of your government, doing very little to collect the taxes owed. Cumulative uncollected tax revenues spanning the last 10 years total over $250 million. Of this amount, we estimate that $128 million will not ever be recovered because of the age of the debt. BIR and DOF have focused on accounting for receipts and ignored their charge to collect delinquent taxes. Specifically, they did not (1) always timely assess taxpayers, (2) identify non-filers, (3) meet collection timelines, or (4) focus collection efforts to maximize recovery. These conditions, taken collectively, demonstrate a systematic breakdown in the collection of delinquent taxes, which undermines the integrity of the Virgin Islands tax system. The conditions are of long-standing and have been documented in numerous reports (see Appendix 2).

We also found agency practices that circumvented legislation enacted to prevent tax evasion through the use of tax clearance letters and the abuse of position by an official charged with enforcing the legislation. Under the law, the Department of Licensing and Consumer Affairs (DLCA) and BIR form a system of checks and balances to ensure that business licenses are not issued to applicants with delinquent taxes. However, DLCA issued business licenses to applicants who did not have tax clearance letters, and BIR issued clearance letters when delinquent taxes were owed. These practices rendered the tax evasion legislation ineffective and further undermined the integrity of GVI's tax collection efforts. In the case of BIR, the former Director, between 2002 and 2006, issued 237 favorable tax clearance letters to taxpayers, some of whom were not current in their filing and paying of taxes or did not have a payment agreement in place. The letters to delinquent taxpayers falsely stated that, according to BIR, the taxpayers were current in filing and paying their tax obligations, thereby allowing them to evade payment of taxes to GVI.

Given the breadth and depth of tax collection deficiencies, we concluded that your direct intervention is needed to achieve significant and lasting improvements. Accordingly, our five recommendations represent a holistic approach to correcting deficiencies and provide an opportunity, as you begin your new administration, to establish an effective and vigorous tax collection process that maximizes the revenues needed to support the work of your administration. We are pleased that you agree with our recommendations, as stated in your November 30, 2007 response to our draft report (Appendix 4). Based on your response, we consider Recommendations 1, 2, and 4 to be resolved but not implemented and Recommendations 3 and 5 to be resolved and implemented (Appendix 5).

The legislation, as amended, creating the Office of Inspector General requires that we report to Congress semiannually on all audit reports issued, the monetary effect of audit findings, actions taken to implement our audit recommendations, and recommendations that have not been implemented. The monetary impact of the findings in this report is shown in Appendix 3.

Please provide a response to this report by February 28, 2008. The response should provide the information requested in Appendix 5 and be addressed to Mr. Hannibal M. Ware, Field Office Supervisor, Office of Inspector General, Caribbean Field Office, Ron deLugo Federal Building, Room 207, St. Thomas, VI 00802. We appreciate the cooperation shown by government staff during our audit. If you have any questions concerning this report, you may contact me at (916) 978-5653 or Mr. Hannibal M. Ware at (340) 774-8300.

Sincerely,

Michael P. Colombo
Regional Audit Manager

Enclosure

cc: Director, Bureau of Internal Revenue
Commissioner, Department of Finance

CONTENTS

Acronyms

BIR.. Bureau of Internal Revenue
DLCA .... Department of Licensing and Consumer Affairs
DOF ....Department of Finance
OIG .... U.S. Department of the Interior, Office of Inspector General
GVI ....Government of the Virgin Islands
VIC .... Virgin Islands Code

INTRODUCTION

GOVERNMENT, ECONOMY, AND REVENUES

The Virgin Islands are an unincorporated territory of the United States, located about 1,000 miles southeast of Miami, Florida. The U.S. Department of the Interior assumed responsibility for administration of the Virgin Islands in 1931, and in 1936 the U.S. Congress enacted the Organic Act, which established the Islands' civil government. The Revised Organic Act of 1954 established a state constitution. The economy of the Virgin Islands is based on tourism and industries, such as rum production, oil refining, and jewelry manufacturing.

In fiscal year 2007, GVI's revenue budget totaled about $917 million, of which about $689 million was local revenues. Local tax revenue accounts for 75 percent of the funds available for expenditure by GVI, as shown in Figure 1 below.

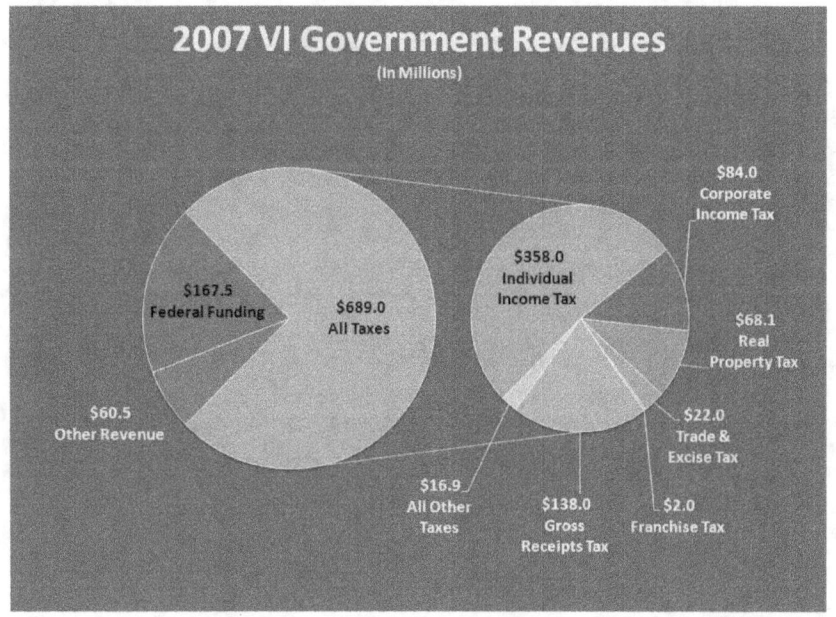

Figure 1

As a U.S. Territory, GVI is subject, with few exceptions, to U.S. federal rules and regulations, including the U.S. Internal Revenue Code. The booklet, Tax Structure of the U.S. Virgin Islands, prepared by the Office of the Chief Counsel for BIR, states:

> The sources of the Virgin Islands taxing authority include the Internal Revenue Code of 1986 . . . and the Naval Service Appropriations Act of 1922, which established the principle that the IRC [U.S. Internal Revenue Code] applies in the Virgin Islands under a 'MIRROR SYSTEM' whereby the 'VIRGIN ISLANDS' is substituted for the 'UNITED STATES' whenever necessary.

BIR and DOF[1] are the two primary agencies responsible for collecting the tax revenues necessary to finance the obligations of GVI. BIR is charged with collecting personal and corporate income taxes, payroll withholding taxes, gross receipts taxes, and hotel occupancy taxes. DOF is responsible for collecting all real property taxes and sewer fees, as assessed, prepared, and recorded by the Lieutenant Governor's Office.

With a history of tax administration and collection problems, GVI, in 1985, enacted tax evasion legislation to be implemented by the Lieutenant Governor's Office, DLCA, and BIR.[2] Under this legislation, DLCA cannot issue or renew a license to do business in the Virgin Islands without an affidavit, known as the tax clearance letter, signed by BIR affirming that all taxes have been paid or that an agreement to pay outstanding taxes has been made. Since passage of this legislation, however, minimal progress has been made in collecting tax revenues from delinquent taxpayers and non-filers.

---

[1] Responsibilities for both agencies are authorized under the Virgin Islands Code (VIC): 33 VIC § 681 for the BIR and 33 VIC § 2492 for the DOF.
[2] 27 VIC § 304

RESULTS OF AUDIT

The failure to address identified long-standing deficiencies in the collection of delinquent taxes continues a decade-long practice of administrative non-feasance. BIR and DOF did very little to collect from delinquent taxpayers and non-filers, resulting in over $250 million (Figure 2) in cumulative uncollected tax revenues over the past 10 years, of which an estimated $128 million is not likely to be collected. This occurred because BIR and DOF focused on accounting for receipts to the exclusion of collection efforts. In addition, we found circumvention of law in the issuance of business licenses to applicants who were delinquent in paying taxes, and in one instance we found a flagrant abuse of position in the issuance of tax clearance letters. These conditions, taken collectively, demonstrate a systematic breakdown in the collection of delinquent taxes, which undermines the integrity of the Virgin Islands tax system.

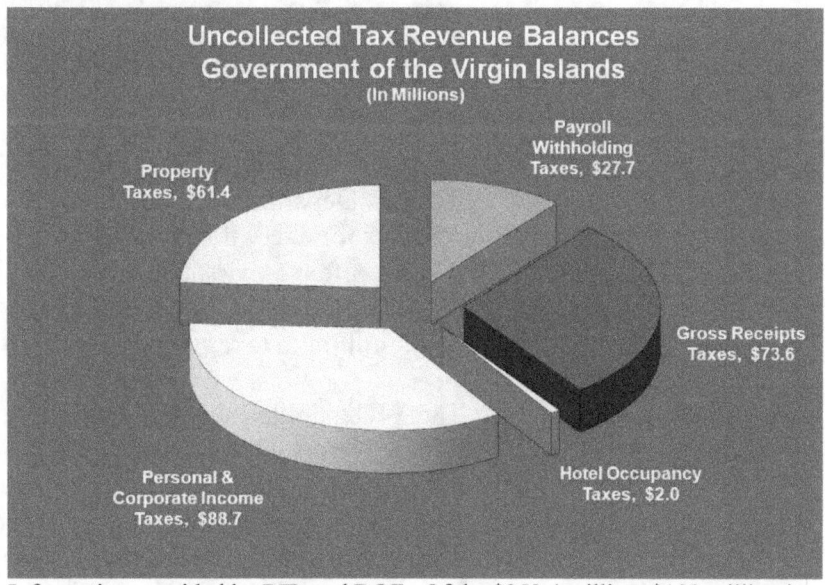

Information provided by BIR and DOF. Of the $253.4 million, $192 million is revenue that would have been collected by BIR and $61.4 million by DOF.

Figure 2

BIR COLLECTION ACTIVITIES UNFOCUSED

We reviewed 160 taxpayer accounts consisting of 40 personal and corporate income tax accounts, 40 gross receipts tax accounts, 40 payroll tax withholding accounts, and 40 hotel occupancy tax accounts representing $23.5 million of the $192 million owed. We found significant deficiencies in tax collection practices that illustrated BIR's failure to discharge its tax collection responsibilities to maximize tax collection. Specifically, BIR did not (1) timely assess taxpayers, (2) meet collection timelines, (3) effectively use collection officers, or (4) identify non-filers. As a result of the age of the debt (Figure 3), we estimate that

$128 million of the $192 million in uncollected tax revenue is not likely to be collected, a potential waste of financial resources that could have been used by GVI.

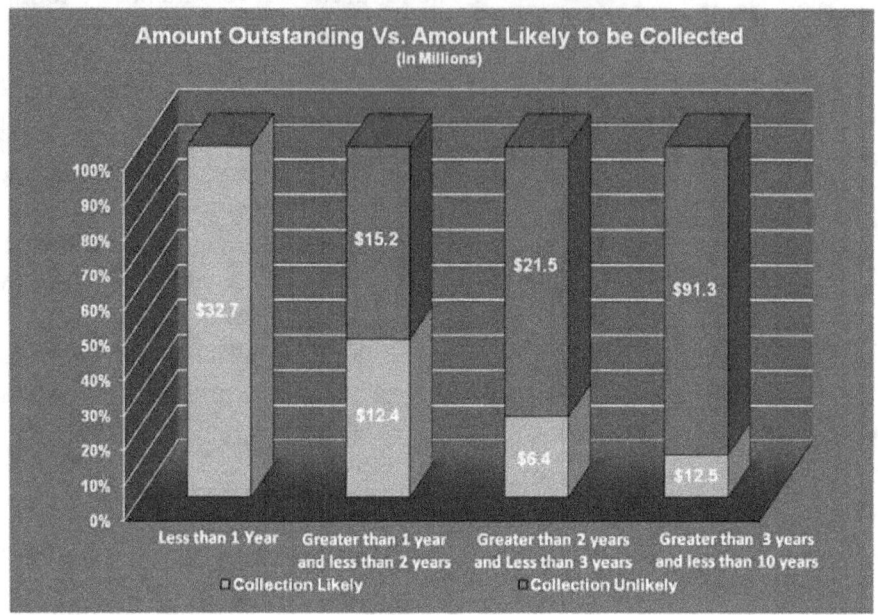

Figure 3

The older the debt, the less likely it will be collected. According to the U.S. Department of Commerce, collection is reduced to 45 cents for every dollar owed on a 1-year delinquent debt; to 23 cents after 2 years; and to 12 cents after 3 years. Using this formula, BIR, at best, will collect only one-third of the $192 million in taxes owed.

▶**Untimely Tax Assessments**

The VIC[3] stipulates that all internal revenue taxes must be assessed within 3 years after a return is filed. Assessments begin the tax collection process, and if an assessment is not made within 3 years, BIR cannot legally collect the tax. We found 20 instances in our sample of 160 taxpayer accounts where BIR did not assess within the mandated time frame, resulting in the loss of $731,904 in owed taxes.

Additionally, BIR did not initiate the collection process for tax returns submitted without full payment until an average of 18 months had elapsed, thereby squandering half of the 3-year period allowed for tax assessment under the VIC. By taking 18 months to make an assessment of taxes, BIR's likely collection rate is significantly reduced from 100 percent to 45 percent, as illustrated in Figure 3.

---

[3] 33 VIC § 1161

▶ Failure to Meet Collection Time Lines

Even after making assessments, BIR neglected to issue delinquent notices according to established procedures, which require BIR to issue three such notices within 90 days to remind taxpayers that payment is due and that property could be seized for payment. After 90 days, BIR should prepare a delinquency report, which is used to assign cases to revenue officers for collection. We found that BIR did not send second and third notices to 129 of the 160 taxpayers sampled that were delinquent for periods of up to 5 years. According to BIR officials, the mechanism for issuing second and third notices was disabled in 2004 because of (1) insufficient capacity on the tax computer system and (2) a large number of errors related to a changeover from an older computer system, which caused incorrect notices to be issued to taxpayers. Because BIR discontinued issuing second and third notices, the tax system no longer generated delinquency reports. Without these reports, the Chief of Delinquent Accounts and Returns stated that she began assigning cases based on high dollar values. However, our testing revealed that cases were not assigned systematically. In fact, of the 160 taxpayer accounts reviewed, 109, valued at $13.7 million, had never been assigned to revenue officers for collection, although some had been assessed as far back as 1997.

▶ Ineffective Use of Revenue Officers

We also noted that revenue officers allocated a significant amount of time researching the validity of taxpayer delinquencies when delinquency notices were issued. Because the Chief of Delinquent Accounts and Returns signs the delinquency notices issued by the Processing Accounts and Returns Branch, taxpayers with questions about the notices come directly to revenue officers, rather than going to processing personnel. As a result, according to revenue officers, they functioned more as "correction" rather than "collection" officers, working to correct errors, which included missing payments and tax exemption credits issued by the Economic Development Commission.[4]

In cases where revenue officers attempted to collect taxes due on assigned cases, BIR's failure to follow through on enforcement of liens and other collection devices rendered these attempts ineffective. For example:

➢ A contractor owed $960,190 in withholding taxes from March 2002 through April 2007. Although revenue officers filed three different liens in 2001 and 2004, BIR did not enforce the liens, even though withholding tax is a federal tax for which nonpayment can result in imprisonment. After years of BIR's inaction, the liens were rendered unenforceable.

---

[4] The Economic Development Commission was established to encourage business expansion in the Virgin Islands and can grant a variety of tax benefits, including tax exemptions.

> A hotel owed hotel occupancy taxes of almost $100,000 since 2000. In 2006, when BIR found out the hotel property was to be sold by auction, it prepared a summons and a lien. However, the lien was filed only 15 days before the property was sold for $900,000, and BIR was unable to collect any of the outstanding taxes.

▶ **No Enforcement of Collection from Non-Filers**

BIR did not make any effort to identify non-filers until our audit began and therefore had no assurance that all entities required to file taxes in the Virgin Islands were doing so. BIR has the capability to identify non-filers of personal income taxes, based on W-2s and 1099s provided by employers, detailing the amount of wages paid. However, BIR did not take timely action to identify non-filers and collect taxes when warranted. We found that 18,669 W-2 and 1099 information returns for tax years 2003 and 2004, representing over $221 million in wages, could not be matched to any filed tax returns. Of those non-filers, 5,609 W-2s and 1099s were related to GVI employees, with reported earnings of over $83 million. Although BIR was aware of the non-filers, it did not take action to ensure that they filed or that appropriate penalties were applied to the accounts.

Further, BIR undertook only minimal effort to determine the level of non-filers in other tax classifications. For example, we noted that although a doctor filed a single withholding tax return in 2002, we found no evidence that other withholding tax returns were filed or paid, even though this doctor continued to operate a practice at the time of our audit. We found no evidence of any activities undertaken by BIR to determine why the doctor had not filed since 2002. Without canvassing or crosschecking the different classes of taxes, BIR could not ensure that all businesses required to file were actually filing.

REAL PROPERTY TAX BILLS UNPAID WITHOUT CONSEQUENCE

In addition to our sample of 160 deliquent accounts at BIR, we also sampled 80 delinquent property tax accounts totaling $9.4 million at DOF and found no evidence of effective collection effort. The lack of effort occurred because (1) DOF's manual tax and payment recording systems did not provide accurate and up-to-date taxpayer information, and (2) DOF did not make a sustained effort to collect outstanding taxes. As a result, $61.4 million in unpaid property taxes and penalties is currently owed GVI[5].

▶ **Antiquated Recordkeeping Practices**

The process of determining outstanding property tax balances was cumbersome and time consuming and did not lend itself to the efficient or effective collection of taxes. To determine the total delinquency of a taxpayer who has not paid property taxes for more than 1 tax year, enforcement officers must compile a status

---

[5] For all property tax periods up to 2004.

report that lists the annual delinquency of the taxpayer. This entails manually researching copies of old bills located in file cabinets and determining the amount owed by reviewing dusty, old, and hard-to-read annual tax rolls stacked on shelves at DOF (see Figure 4).

Figure 4

After completion of manual research, which also includes determining whether Economic Development Commission tax exemption credits have been accurately applied, enforcement officers must consult the Real Property Tax Inquiry System to find out whether payments for prior years have been made. When enforcement officers have compiled the amount of taxes owed, they must then manually calculate related penalties and fees.

This time-consuming process hindered collection efforts because enforcement officers and collectors had to allocate a significant amount of time to researching taxpayer delinquencies, rather than actually collecting taxes. In addition we found an example of understaffing at one of DOF's enforcement offices. Specifically, the St. Croix office was understaffed, with only one enforcement officer and two collectors assigned to handle delinquencies, resulting in low morale and poor collection efforts. We were told that retired enforcement officers were contracted to prepare and issue status reports to delinquent taxpayers. However, we were unable to determine what, if anything, was done by these contractors because DOF could not locate documentation showing their efforts.

► **Minimal Efforts Equals No Results**

Based on our review of 80 delinquent tax accounts, we found that collection efforts consisted of one letter notifying a taxpayer of unpaid taxes and three instances where taxpayer names were published in newspapers. The VIC stipulates:

> Within sixty (60) days after the date on which taxes and public sewer user fees become delinquent [tax bills become delinquent 60 days after they become due], the Commissioner of Finance shall publish the names of all delinquent real property tax owners once in a different newspaper of general circulation in each

island district, and such publication shall be deemed as notice to the taxpayer of the impending sale of the real property at public auction. Said general notice shall state that unless such delinquent taxes and public sewer system user fees, together with the interest provided by section 2393 of this title, are paid within a period of 30 days from the publication date of the said notice, the property of the taxpayer will be attached and sold in a manner provided in this subtitle.

Further review disclosed that DOF published delinquent taxpayer notices only for property taxes due prior to 1997 and has not had a sale of property to satisfy a tax debt since 2005. These efforts fall far short of what is needed to recover the delinquent property tax debt of $61.4 million.

CIRCUMVENTION OF LAW AND ABUSE OF POSITION

Twenty-two years after the Virgin Islands legislature passed legislation to prevent tax evasion, we discovered the circumvention of this legislation and the abuse of power by an official charged with enforcement of the law. DLCA's issuance of business licenses without tax clearance letters and BIR's issuance of clearance letters when delinquent taxes were owed rendered the tax evasion legislation ineffective and further undermined the integrity of GVI's tax collection efforts.

The Virgin Islands legislature envisioned that the use of affidavits, known as tax clearance letters, would be an integral part of a program to prevent tax evasion. As part of initial applications for business licenses, tax clearance letters were "gatekeepers," that is, business license applications could not be accepted by DLCA without favorable letters. The VIC[6] states:

> (j) The Commissioner [of DLCA] shall not issue or renew a license to do business to any person who fails to present at the time of application for said license or renewal affidavits signed by an authorized officer of the Virgin Islands Bureau of Internal Revenue and the Division of Corporation and Trademark, Office of the Lieutenant Governor affirming that said applicant has filed and paid all taxes, penalties, and interest applicable to said business or any other other business venture including a certification from the corporate division of the Lieutenant Governor's office that all franchise taxes have been paid, or has satisfactorily made agreement to pay the same.

> (k) The Commissioner shall, after ten (10) days' notice, revoke any license of a person who fails to file and pay all taxes, penalties, and interest due to the Virgin Islands Bureau of Internal Revenue and the Division of Corporations and Trademarks, Office of the Lieutenant

---

[6] 27 VIC § 304

Governor in connection with the operation of his business activities or who has not made a satisfactory agreement to pay the same.

We were told that DLCA, acting alone and contrary to the law, established an internal policy that allows only 15 working days for receipt of a tax clearance letter before DLCA will issue a license anyway. This practice creates an environment that at best fails to prevent tax evasion and at worst encourages and abets it.

We found eight instances where taxpayers obtained current business licenses without obtaining a tax clearance letter from BIR and three additional instances where, despite unfavorable tax clearance letters from BIR, taxpayers were granted current business licenses. In one of these instances, the applicant received a business license after receiving an unfavorable letter from BIR for $3.5 million in unpaid gross receipts and withholding taxes.

▶Abuse of Position by Former BIR Director

The former Director of BIR abused his position when he issued favorable tax clearance letters to delinquent taxpayers, circumventing control procedures established under the VIC[7] and thereby aiding and abetting the nonpayment of delinquent taxes.

Tax clearance letters were to be issued only after researching all accounts on the tax system to determine whether the taxpayer was current or delinquent. In 2002, after the Supervisor of Tax Records issued an unfavorable letter to a contractor owing $435,000 in delinquent taxes, the former Director disregarded the unfavorable letter and issued a favorable tax clearance letter which he signed for the supervisor. The former Director continued to issue favorable letters to the contractor through 2005, with the contractor owing GVI $437,000 in delinquent gross receipts and withholding taxes.

Between 2002 and 2006, the former Director issued 237 favorable tax clearance letters to taxpayers, some of whom were not current in their filing and paying of taxes or did not have a payment agreement in place. The letters to delinquent taxpayers falsely stated that, according to BIR, the taxpayers were current in filing and paying their tax obligations, thereby allowing them to evade payment of taxes to GVI. For example, we found 31 favorable tax clearance letters issued to a businessperson who owned a chain of 31 gas stations and convenient stores on St. Croix. The businessperson had evaded filing and payment of taxes to the St. Croix office for 7 years, despite efforts by a revenue officer and managers in that office to collect the taxes through summons,

---

[7] The VIC provides that BIR may issue tax clearance letters to taxpayers who are either current on their tax liabilities or who have established and are current on a tax payment plan.

director returns, liens, and levies. The businessperson eventually accumulated a balance of $1.75 million in taxes owed for 21 of the 31 businesses for which tax returns were filed.[8] When the management of the St. Croix office refused to issue favorable tax clearance letters to the businessperson, the businessperson traveled to St. Thomas, where the former Director issued favorable letters in May 2004 for a one-time payment of $25,000. We have referred this abuse by the former Director to our Office of Investigations.

---

[8] The businessperson did not file returns for the remaining 10 businesses.

RECOMMENDATIONS

We recommend that the Governor of the Virgin Islands:

1. Lead a tax administration task force to develop an action plan ensuring filing and payment of all taxes due GVI. This task force should include directors and commissioners of tax collection authorities and other tax experts from outside GVI. Issues to be addressed should include integrating and focusing tax administration and collection efforts GVI-wide and establishing staffing levels for effective tax program performance.

2. Direct BIR and DOF to develop a plan and process to correct taxpayer accounts to allow for timely tax status determination and collection activities.

3. Direct BIR and DOF to establish tax assessment and delinquency notification processes to ensure timely communication of taxes due and enforcement and collection action on delinquent accounts. Actions would include assessing all taxes, issuing collection notices, and assigning tax debts to revenue officers in a timely manner to minimize tax revenue losses.

4. Direct BIR to begin matching W-2 and 1099 forms to individual and corporate returns to identify potential non-filers, assess tax liabilities based on available information, and initiate immediate collection actions to encourage filing as well as collecting revenues due.

5. Direct BIR to discontinue issuing tax clearance letters to any taxpayers who are not current in their tax payments or who do not have tax payment agreements in force.

GOVERNOR'S
RESPONSE AND
OFFICE OF
INSPECTOR
GENERAL (OIG)
REPLY

In his November 30, 2007 response to our draft report (Appendix 4), the Governor of the Virgin Islands concurred with our recommendations. The Governor stated that his office was "already in the planning stages of acquiring the consultants needed from outside the GVI to work with BIR management and staff as a 'working' task force to enhance our internal focus on tax and fee administration." The Governor also stated that "a ten (10) point plan to address the items that have been identified by both this audit and the BIR already has been drafted," including freeing up and empowering revenue officers to "aggressively" pursue delinquent collection from delinquent taxpayers, identifying non-filers, and working with DLCA to prevent tax evasion. In addition, as part of his response, the Governor provided information showing that BIR and DOF had implemented plans of action to address each recommendation.

We are heartened both by the Governor's concurrence with our recommendations and by his timeliness in initiating the actions needed to establish an effective and vigorous tax collection process within the Virgin Islands—one that maximizes the revenues needed to effectively operate the government. We look forward to receiving continued confirmation of this ongoing work. Based on the Governor's response, we consider Recommendations 1, 2, and 4 to be resolved but not implemented and Recommendations 3 and 5 to be resolved and implemented. The status of the audit recommendations is shown in Appendix 5.

Appendix 1 - Audit Scope and Methodology

The objective of our audit was to identify the current level of taxes and fees owed to GVI and determine if GVI was making reasonable efforts to collect these outstanding amounts. We judgmentally sampled and reviewed 160 delinquent accounts totaling $23.5 million at BIR for tax years 2003 to 2005 and 80 delinquent property tax accounts totaling $9.4 million at DOF from the 2004 delinquency list, based on the dollar amount of the delinquent accounts.

We performed our audit work from September 2006 through June 2007. To accomplish our objective, we interviewed officials and reviewed tax forms, payment records, computerized tax information, collection history files, tax clearance letters, annual tax bills, and tax rolls on St. Thomas and St. Croix. We also consulted with officials from DLCA, the Lieutenant Governor's office on St. Thomas and St. Croix, and the Economic Development Commission on St. Thomas.

Our audit was conducted in accordance with the *Government Auditing Standards*, issued by the Comptroller General of the United States. Accordingly, we included such tests of records and other auditing procedures we considered necessary under the circumstances. As part of the audit, we evaluated the internal controls related to the administration and collection of personal and corporate income, gross receipts, hotel occupancy, withholding, and real property taxes and sewer fees to the extent we considered necessary to accomplish the audit objective.

Our evaluation disclosed significant internal control deficiencies that called into question the accuracy of the taxes owed. BIR and DOF did not always ensure that payments were applied timely to taxpayer accounts or that tax information was reconciled. In addition, BIR and DOF incorrectly categorized some tax exempt accounts as delinquent accounts, causing receivables to be overstated by at least $6.5 million.

We found 46 instances where BIR did not apply payments to taxpayer accounts until after 1 to 6 years had elapsed. Further, when BIR transferred gross receipts and hotel occupancy taxes from its old stand-alone systems to the Virgin Islands Tax System in 2004, all data were not thoroughly reconciled prior to the transfer.

The Virgin Islands Tax System did not always contain updated and reconciled information, nor did BIR maintain reliable and

13

accessible hard copies of tax returns to ensure the validity of taxpayer information. Of the 160 taxpayer accounts reviewed, we found that original tax returns for 90 accounts, valued at $9.8 million, could not be readily retrieved.

Given the magnitude of the control and recording deficiencies identified, we were unable to determine the financial effects such deficiencies had on the tax receivable balances. Internal control weaknesses identified as a result of our audit are discussed in the Results of Audit section of this report. The recommendations, if implemented, should improve the internal controls in tax collection.

Appendix 2 – Prior Audit Coverage

Over the past 20 years, we have performed a number of audits and evaluations of various aspects of GVI's tax collection process. Common to each of these reports are deficiencies that collectively demonstrate a systemic breakdown in tax administration and enforcement, which undermines public confidence in the fair administration of GVI's tax laws. Our reports in these areas include the following:

➤ August 2003, *Follow-up of Recommendation Relating to Internal Revenue Taxes, Bureau of Internal Revenue, Government of the Virgin Islands* (No. 2003-I-0059) BIR did not take action to (1) collect $4.8 million from delinquent taxpayers; (2) collect a total of $408,000 from 68 delinquent accounts before the statute of limitations expired; and (3) file liens and levies on delinquent taxpayers to serve as the government's claim against their property.

➤ March 1999, *Administration of Real Property Taxes, Government of the Virgin Islands* (No. 99-I-379) DOF did not maintain accounts receivable records for delinquent real property tax bills or effectively enforce the collection of delinquent taxes. GVI revenue accounts were also not up to date because of delays in posting property tax collections. We estimated that delinquent property taxes totaled at least $15.4 million.

➤ December 1997, *Internal Revenue Taxes, Bureau of Internal Revenue, Government of the Virgin Islands* (No. 98-I-188) BIR did not (1) realize all potential revenue collections because it could not access a taxpayer's complete and accurate payment history for all classes of taxes from a single computer system; (2) effectively use collection practices and tools, such as liens and levies, to enforce the collection of amounts owed by taxpayers; or (3) implement adequate internal controls to effectively administer its audit function. BIR also did not collect $10.1 million from over 1,700 taxpayer cases or $324,000 because the statute of limitations had expired and had granted penalty waivers totaling $795,000 without required documentation. In addition, data produced by the Computer Operations Branch to detect and prevent non-filers and filers of duplicate dependent claims were not made available to the Audit Enforcement Branch in a consistent and timely manner.

➤ May 1991, *Follow-up of Recommendations Regarding Gross Receipts, Hotel Occupancy, Excise, and Income Taxes, Government of the Virgin Islands* (No. 91-I-791)
Many of the deficiencies disclosed in the prior reports still existed and could be attributed to underlying problems. These problems must be corrected before BIR can effectively administer, enforce, and collect taxes.

➤ April 1990, *Follow-up of Recommendations Concerning Property Tax Administration Activities, Government of the Virgin Islands* (No. 90-67)
DOF could enhance efficiency, increase revenues, and reduce the risk of property tax losses by improving collection procedures and did not have adequate control over the records and processes used to enforce property tax collection.

➤ February 1988, *Administration, Enforcement, and Collection of Property Taxes, Government of the Virgin Islands* (No. 88-46)
Improvements were needed in the overall administration of income taxes, the ability to locate and identify delinquent taxpayers, the level of effort exercised in collecting delinquent taxes, and the internal controls over actual tax collections.

Appendix 3 – Monetary Impact

Finding Area	Uncollected Revenues	Wasted Revenues	Potentially Lost Revenues
	(In Millions)		
LACK OF COLLECTION EFFORTS – BIR (Recommendation 3)			
Subtotal	$192.0	$0.7[1]	$128.0[2]
LACK OF COLLECTION EFFORTS – DOF (Recommendation 3)			
Subtotal	$61.4		
Total	**$253.4**		

[1] Of the $253.4 million, $0.7 million cannot be collected because BIR did not assess the taxes within the legally mandated time frame.

[2] Based on the age of the debt, an estimated $128 million is potentially uncollectible.

17

Appendix 4 – Governor of the Virgin Islands' Response

THE UNITED STATES VIRGIN ISLANDS

OFFICE OF THE GOVERNOR
GOVERNMENT HOUSE
Charlotte Amalie, V.I. 00802
340-774-0001

November 30, 2007

Ms. Kimberly Elmore
Acting Assistant Inspector General for Audits
U. S. Department of the Interior
1849 C Street, NW, MS 5341
Washington, D.C. 20240

RE: Response by the Government of the Virgin Islands to Draft Report
Collection of Outstanding Taxes and Fees, Government of the Virgin
Islands Assignment No. V-IN-VIS-0011-2006, October 2007

Dear Ms. Elmore:

The purpose of this correspondence is twofold. First, is to acknowledge receipt of the above-referenced draft audit report, which was transmitted by Mr. Michael P. Colombo, Regional Audit Manager in his letter dated October 5, 2007. Second, is to provide you with my response to your report and specifically to your recommendations.

The report finds that the Government of the Virgin Islands (GVI) Bureau of Internal Revenue (BIR) and Department of Finance (DOF) must substantially improve the collection of delinquent taxes and systematically improve the GVI's overall revenue collection results. I concur with your findings.

This report is timely. At the beginning of my administration, my staff and I concluded that the subject of tax and fee revenue collection, processing and policy would be a prime focus as we move forward. Some of this work has already begun. As an example, I have sent legislation to the Senate, which was recently passed to transfer the Property Tax collection process to the Lieutenant Governor's Office (Tax Assessor's Office) which we believe, will enhance the collection of real property taxes. Additionally my staff has drafted a ten (10) point plan to address many of the concerns raised in your audit. These types of initiatives will be the cornerstone of ensuring that our revenue programs meet or exceed the standards we have set for excellence.

Attached you will find the corrective action response to each of the recommendations you have offered, including the person responsible and the due date or implementation date. Thank you for affording the GVI the opportunity to comment on your draft audit report.

Sincerely,

John P. de Jongh, Jr.
Governor

pc: Mr. Hannibal M. Ware
Field Office Supervisor, DOI-OIG
Director, Bureau of Internal Revenue
Commissioner, Department of Finance
Director, Department of Licensing and Consumer Affairs
Director, Office of Management and Budget

RESPONSE TO RECOMMENDATIONS

<u>Recommendation No. 1</u>

We recommend that the Governor of the Virgin Islands lead a tax administration task force to develop an action plan ensuring filing and payment of all taxes due GVI. This task force should include directors and commissioners of tax collection authorities and other tax experts from outside the GVI. Issues to be addressed should include integrating and focusing tax administration and collection efforts GVI-wide and establishing staffing levels for effective tax program performance.

GOVERNMENT'S RESPONSE:

The GVI agrees with this recommendation.

The Governor's Office is already in the planning stages of acquiring the consultants needed from outside the GVI to work with BIR management and staff as a "working" task force to enhance our internal focus on tax and fee administration. The Governor's Office will enable this "working" task force to look at policy and practice in conjunction with processing to ensure we have an adequate system in place to manage the rules and regulations that are set forth by the legislative and administrative bodies and which addresses the concerns raised in this audit. Also, a ten (10) point plan to address the items that have been identified by both this audit and the BIR already has been drafted. The points are:

1. Consolidate "clean-up" work in the Division of Accounts Receivable to a small unit of employees in each office, freeing Revenue Officers (RO) and Revenue Representatives (Rev Reps) to undertake field enforcement work on their inventories. The unit would be knowledgeable and responsible for performing non-RO and non-Rev Rep work (clearly defined). This would provide for a less expensive way to get the "clean-up" work performed and allow RO's to do required enforcement field work.

2. Empower and require Revenue Officers and available Revenue Representatives to manage inventory of presumed valid delinquent accounts through aggressive collection and enforcement actions, employing enforcement tools in a firm but fair manner.

3. Initiate a Compliance Program focused on Virgin Islands Government Employees to identify non-filers and delinquent payers, coordinating enforcement efforts with Government Agency Heads, GVI Personnel Division, and the Department of

Finance's Payroll Division; Government House will assure interagency cooperation.

4. Initiate a Compliance Program focused on Corporations and other large employers to identify non-filers and delinquent payers, to include initiatives addressing specific industries known to be non-compliant (including contractors on all three islands).

5. Finance the upgrade of the computer processing system to begin a matching program for W-2's and 1099's to identify non-filers and under-reporters.

6. Identify and train one Revenue Officer in each District to assume the role of "Compromise Specialist" to manage and advise on all Settlement Offers and payment plans proposed by delinquent taxpayers.

7. Initiate action with the Department of Licensing and Consumer Affairs to assure proper and lawful administration of the Stop Tax Evasion Program (STEP) between DLCA and BIR, and update DLCA's on-line computer program.

8. Arrange for refresher training for RO's and RR's in using enforcement tools in the collection process; periodically conduct CPE.

9. Establish an MOU with IRS (US) to process seizures and sales on the US Mainland for BIR.

10. Modify System to allow utilization of IRS US Levy Sources for VI Delinquent Taxpayers, and to accelerate the implementation of system issuance of 2nd and 3rd Notices.

Person Responsible: Director of the Bureau of Internal Revenue

Implementation Date: October 2007 and ongoing

Recommendation No. 2

We recommend that the Governor of the Virgin Islands direct BIR and DOF to develop a plan and process to correct taxpayer's accounts to allow for timely tax status determination and collection activities.

GOVERNMENT'S RESPONSE:

The GVI agrees with this recommendation.

While the BIR did implement a new tax administration system in 2002 to address the situations cited in the Inspector General's audit, transition to the new system required a more significant conversion process than was anticipated. Some of the challenges regarding account validation following the system conversion primarily stem from (1) the processing of a return and its associated payment on two different systems, (2) taxpayers filing of multiple tax returns for the same tax period, and (3) the administration of the upfront gross receipts tax law. Resolution of these challenges requires a manual review of the account to determine the correct balance due, if any. These challenges are being addressed on a daily basis by the Processing Branch staff. However we recognize that more work is needed.

Delinquent accounts are also being addressed through the issuance of notices and the taxpayers providing proof of payment. The Bureau is in the process of issuing second and third notices in phases to allow an opportunity to correct those accounts that do not properly reflect the taxpayers' full credits. It is anticipated that by March 2008, the automated billing processes for second and third notices will be fully implemented.

DOF concurs and is taking corrective action. The process is currently underway to complete the transfer of the collection of Property Taxes to the Tax Assessor's office under the purview of the Office of the Lieutenant Governor. The consolidation of these functions will improve collections and record keeping as the computer software and data is already in place to accept this responsibility. In the meantime, the Department of Finance is taking steps to intensify the collections processes to minimize the amount of uncollected bills to be transferred.

Person Responsible: Director, Bureau of Internal Revenue
                      Commissioner, Department of Finance
Due Date: April 1, 2008

Recommendation No. 3

We recommend that the Governor of the Virgin Islands direct BIR and DOF to establish tax assessment and delinquency notification processes to ensure timely communication of taxes due and enforcement and collection action on delinquent accounts. Actions would include assessing all taxes, issuing collection notices, and assigning tax debts to revenue officers in a timely manner to minimize tax revenue losses.

GOVERNMENT'S RESPONSE:

The GVI agrees with this recommendation.

BIR's system for processing returns provides for a first notice to be issued once the return is processed and the liability has not been fully paid. The Bureau is in the process of phasing in the full automatic issuance of second and third notices. The current pipeline for processing of tax returns involves first the registration of all returns that enter the BIR followed by the returns being data entered. Once the information on the return is entered, the tax is assessed. The vast majority of tax returns process smoothly through the assessment phase. Returns that have problems that prevent them from being assessed immediately after being data entered are referred to the Error Resolution section to be resolved. This is a manual effort and takes time. The BIR may seek information from the taxpayer, make mathematical or other corrections to the return, and in some cases, may even have to make changes to its software to process the tax return properly and timely.

Despite the procedures that are in place, the BIR concurs that some of these returns are not resolved within the statutory 3-year assessment period. The focus is to minimize untimely processing of tax returns by giving priority to those accounts with statutes that will expire in the current year. In the meantime, BIR's Deputy Director of Operations has issued a memorandum encouraging full compliance until full automation is achieved (see attached).

As noted above, DOF also concurs and the consolidation of Property Tax collection into the Tax Assessor's office is already underway and legal authorization to proceed has been authorized by the Legislature of the Virgin Islands (See proposed legislation attached). Upon receipt by and signature of the Governor a copy of the Act will be transmitted to your office as part of this file.

Person Responsible: Director, Bureau of Internal Revenue
                        Commissioner, Department of Finance
Due Date: BIR - March 31, 2008
                        DOF – March, 2008

Recommendation No. 4

We recommend that the Governor of the Virgin Islands direct BIR to begin matching W2 and 1099 forms to individual and corporate returns to identify potential non-filers, assess tax liabilities based on available information, and initiate immediate collection actions to encourage filing as well as collecting revenues due.

GOVERNMENT RESPONSE:

The GVI agrees with this recommendation.

Funding is not currently budgeted in the FY 2008 budget but will be sought in Fiscal Year 2009 to provide the system enhancements for the Bureau to implement the matching phase of the 1099's and W-2's to the tax return filings.

Persons Responsible: Director, Bureau of Internal Revenue
                        Director, Office of Management and Budget
Due Date: May 1, 2009

Recommendation No. 5

We recommend that the Governor of the Virgin Islands direct BIR to discontinue issuing tax clearance letters to any taxpayers who are not current in their tax payments or who do not have a tax payment agreement in force.

The GVI agrees with this recommendation.

The Governor of the Virgin Islands has directed the Bureau to discontinue utilizing any perceived discretion in the issuance of tax clearance letters. BIR will be required to fully comply with the established procedure pursuant to Virgin Islands law requiring the issuance of a tax clearance to "Stop Tax Evasion" (see attached STEP policy). This includes verification that the taxpayer is current in their tax payments or has a valid tax payment agreement in force. A directive has been sent to the current Director of the Bureau of Internal Revenue reaffirming the support of my administration in not issuing tax clearance letters to delinquent taxpayers who have not paid or who do not have payment plans in place.

A copy of this draft is being forwarded to the Attorney General of the Virgin Islands to review for possible violations of Virgin Islands or Federal Law relative to the issuance of tax clearance as cited in the audit. Additionally, the Commissioner of Licensing and Consumer Affairs has already issued a memorandum to all staff to cease and desist from issuing business licenses without a properly issued tax clearance from BIR (see attached).

Person Responsible: Director, Bureau of Internal Revenue,
Commissioner, Department of Licensing
and Consumer Affairs

Implementation Date: November 12, 2007

Appendix 5 – Status of Audit Recommendations

Finding/ Recommendation Reference	Status	Action Required
1	Resolved, Not Implemented.	We look forward to receiving the written results of the working tax administration task force.
2	Resolved, Not Implemented.	We look forward to receiving a copy of the written plan requested from the Director of BIR.
3 and 5	Resolved and Implemented	None
4	Resolved, Not Implemented.	We look forward to your providing evidence of coordination efforts with other departments to identify employees who are non-filers and action taken to resolve the matter.

Report Fraud, Waste, Abuse And Mismanagement

Fraud, waste, and abuse in government concerns everyone: Office of Inspector General staff, Departmental employees, and the general public. We actively solicit allegations of any inefficient and wasteful practices, fraud, and abuse related to Departmental or Insular area programs and operations. You can report allegations to us in several ways.

By Mail:

U.S. Department of the Interior
Office of Inspector General
Mail Stop 5341 MIB
1849 C Street, NW
Washington, D.C. 20240

By Phone:

24-Hour Toll Free   800-424-5081
Washington Metro Area   703-487-5435

By Fax:

703-487-5402

By Internet:

www.doioig.gov

Revised 07/07